To..Dadd

From..Ruby & Poppy

X X X

Purple Ronnie's

Little Book to say

I ♥ DAD

First published 2011 by Boxtree
an imprint of Pan Macmillan, a division of Macmillan Publishers Limited
Pan Macmillan, 20 New Wharf Road, London N1 9RR
Basingstoke and Oxford
Associated companies throughout the world
www.panmacmillan.com

ISBN 978-0-7522-2726-9

Copyright © Purple Enterprises Ltd, a Coolabi company 2011

9 8 7 6 5 4 3 2 1

A CIP catalogue record for this book is
available from the British Library.

Printed and bound in Hong Kong

'Purple Ronnie' created by Giles Andreae. The right of Giles Andreae and Janet Cronin
to be identified respectively as the author and illustrator of this work has been asserted by them
in accordance with the Copyright, Designs and Patents Act 1988.

Visit **www.panmacmillan.com** to read more about all our books
and to buy them. You will also find features, author interviews and
news of any author events, and you can sign up for e-newsletters
so that you're always first to hear about our new releases.

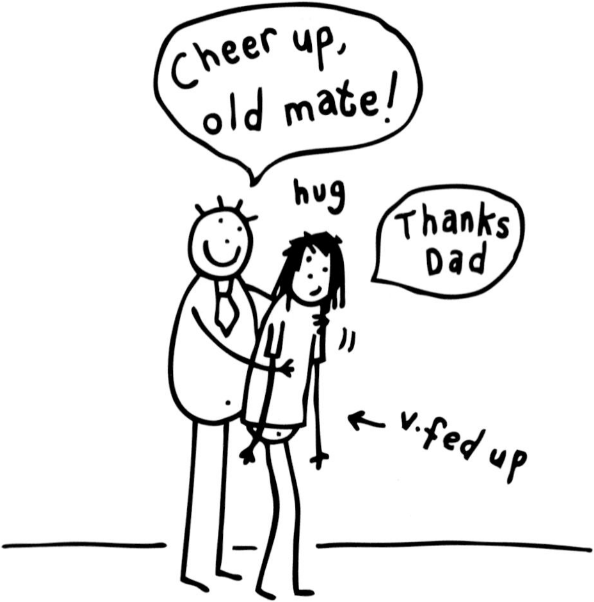
Cheer up, old mate!
hug
Thanks Dad
v. fed up

My Dad, My Hero

You help to lift my
                spirits
When they're dropping
                down to zero
You're there just when
                I need you
Dad-- you are my hero!

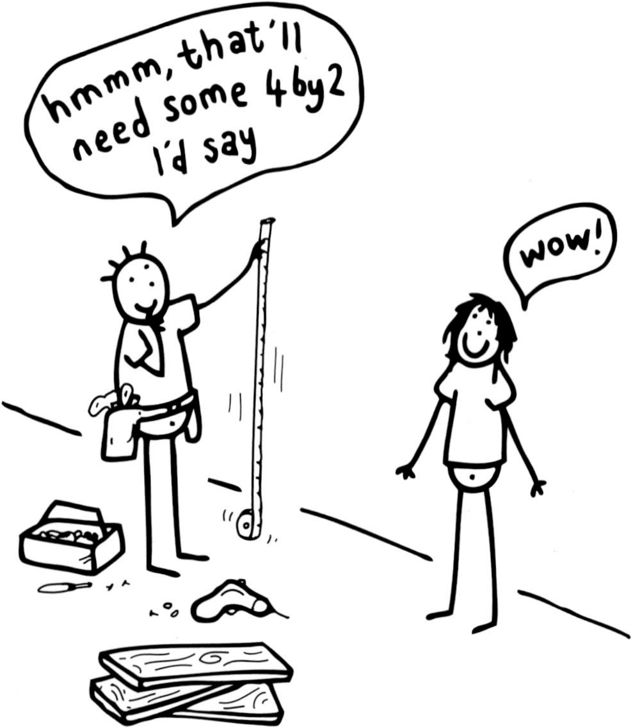
hmmm, that'll need some 4 by 2 I'd say
wow!

D.I.Y. Dad

Some dads can sort
computers out

Some dads can bake a pie,

But my Dad's really clever,

'Cos <u>he</u> does D.I.Y. !

Dad's Hair

Dad's hair has emigrated

It's vanished from his head.

I wonder why it seems to
                    like
His ears and nose instead!

Competitive Dads

Some dads are just naturally competitive

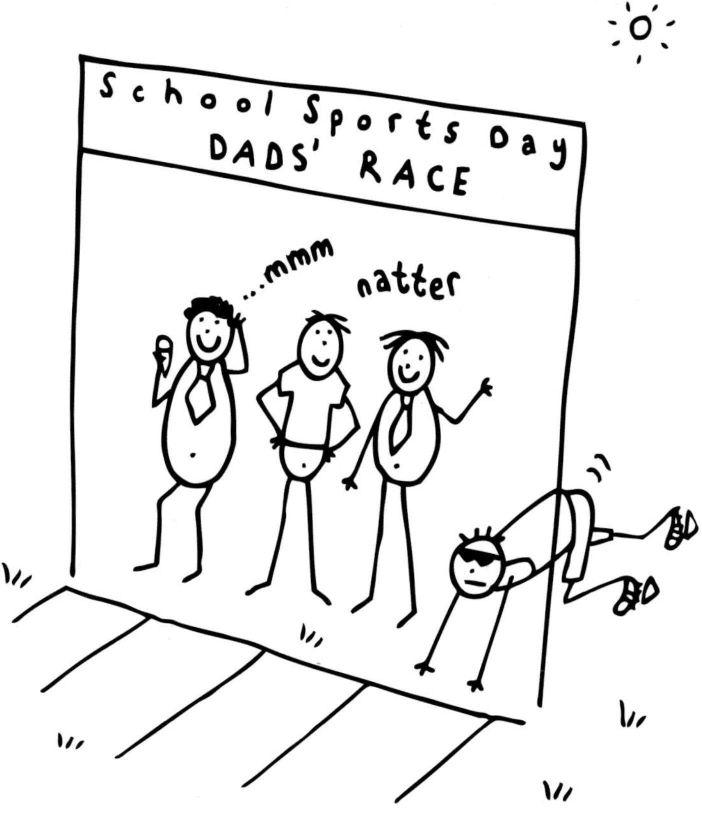
School Sports Day
DADS' RACE
...mmm
natter

In Dad's Day

"When I was young,"
        my Dad drones on,
"We used to have it tough
I had to walk 5 miles to
                    school
In those days things were
            rough"

The Bank of Dad

Dads can be a great source of dosh, if you know how to ask

Erm, Dad, I, uh, really need some stuff for school and things...
wallet bulge

Modern Dad

Our Dad's really Modern,
Into Art and New Design
He's not a beery, blokey
                    dad
He's more like... Food
          and Wine.

Dad of Zen

When Dad is fishing
he falls strangely
silent

Deep calm and focus.
Seeking the Carp
of Enlightenment
v. still

Outdoor Dad

The weather's really fabulous

I'm feeling really glad.

Whoopee I'm in the
                    countryside,

Out camping with my Dad!

Dads and Dating Daughters

Beware of doting dads, young lads,
When trying to date their daughter
They'll check you out so fiercely that
Your knees will turn to water!

...you aint nothin' but a Hound Dog...
bang
bang
Hurry up!
Elvis Kung Fu Kick

Dad in the Bathroom

Dad <u>must</u> know what a
bathroom's for

So why does he forget?

In there he thinks he's
Elvis---

"Hey Dad! You finished yet?"

Dad and Teen Fashion

Dads don't always understand teenage fashions

sigh

Fancy dress party tonight dear...?

Sport
BAD
DAY
NEWS
SCANDAL

I work hard, I deserve a rest
poo-ee, i'm gonna tell Mum
Beer
scratch
NUTS
crisps
Flurb
whiff

Dad Slobs Out

When Mum's away Dad
slobs about
In front of daytime telly
He belches loud, drinks
cans of beer
And pats his hairy belly!

Dad's Fancy Car

Our Dad likes to keep
his car
All shiny, clean and slick
So when he takes us out
in it
It's best to not be sick...!

Dads and Football

It's quite useful to support the same team as your dad

Dad's Music

When we put on our hip-hop

Dad blocks his ears and
groans,

"In _MY_ day we had _MUSIC_:

Pink Floyd and Rolling Stones"

Dad'll Fix It

Dads have an uncanny
knowledge about
mysterious things
like fuseboxes

...You just put the sprocket in the wurzle, flick the gimlet back...
fiddle

Dad the B-B-Q King

Our dad is great at Barbecues.

But when he starts to
party

With all those beers and
burgers down him

Phew! He gets so farty!

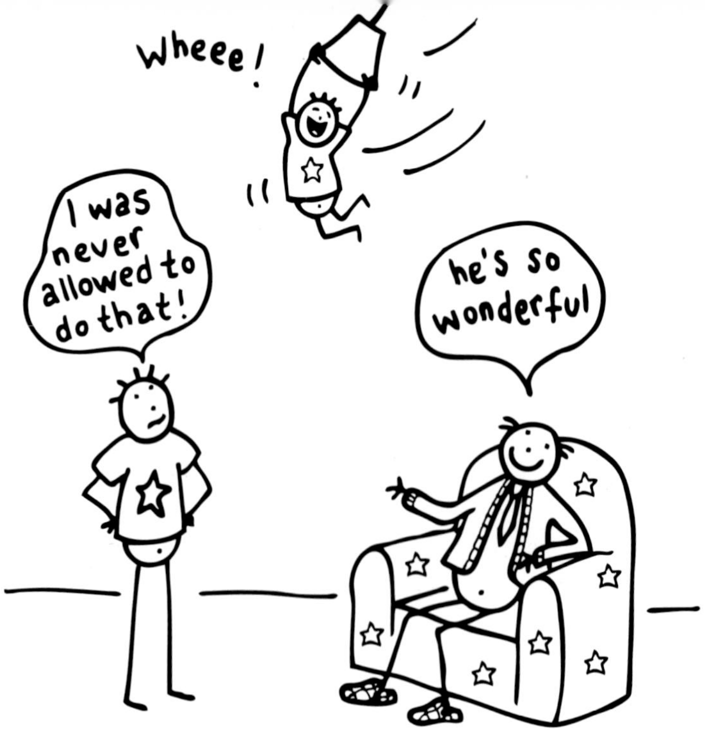
Wheee!
I was never allowed to do that!
he's so wonderful

Dads as Grandads

When dads turn into grandads

They're never half so pushy

When grandkids go to grandads

They get it really cushy!

Dads and Fashion

Dads don't always get it right with clothes. Help them out.

must put some bytes into this memory stack, I think
in heaven
tinker

Gadget Man Dad

I sometimes think that
gadgets
Are simply dad-type toys.
'Cos when dads get their
gadgets out
They're just like little boys!

Minder Dad

Sometimes it's handy to have Dad nearby, in case of trouble

Sporting Dad

Dads often know
better than referees

I used to slip into these like a snake...
oh no!
Don't do it Dad!
heave
squeeze

Dads and Teenagers

Some dads want their
youth back
When their kids grow
into teens.
They try to turn all
trendy
And wear the latest jeans!

Dad Jobs

Some dads are dutiful.
It can keep them busy.

!
Parents' Evening
Son's Footie Match
Lift to Party
Daughter's ballet class
Take bins out
Cut grass
Dad! It's time for my lift to town!

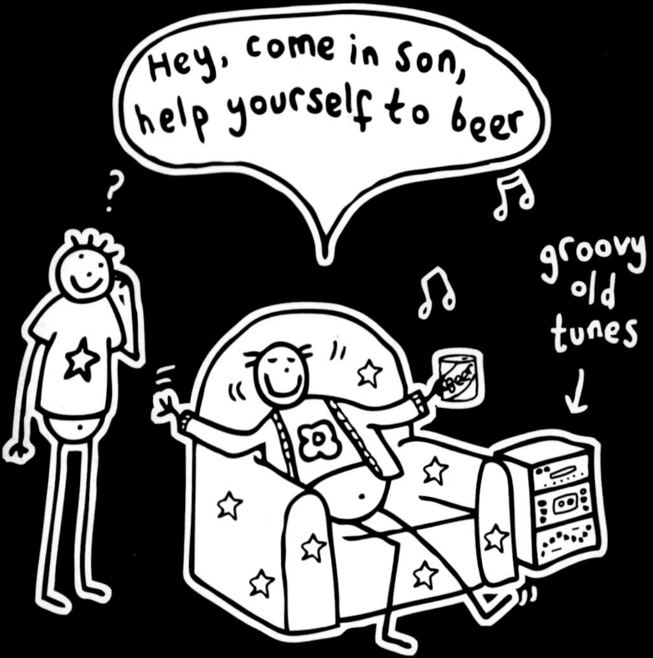
Hey, come in Son,
help yourself to beer
?
groovy
old
tunes
Beer

Laid Back Dad

Some Dads are really
full-on
And keep you right on track.
But my Dad's really easy
going,
Chilled and well
laid-back!

Handy Dad

Hurrah for handy Dad
who taught me
How to change a wheel.
Now when I'm driving
on my own
Flat tyres are no big
deal!

Dad Time

Dads need educating
to keep them up
to date with new
music.

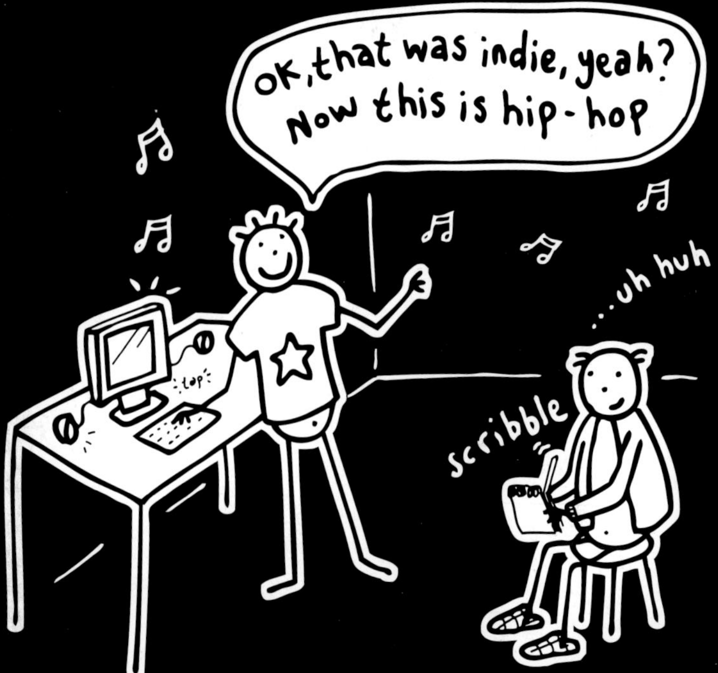
OK, that was indie, yeah? Now this is hip-hop
tap
...uh huh
scribble

That should tide you over for a bit, eh?
urm... I think so
beam
£s
needs more zeros
shuffle

Dad's Cheque Book

When student kids are
stony broke
Nice dads say, "What the
heck..."
They wave their magic
pens about
And scribble out a cheque!

wail... warble... love yoouuu...
...foreeverer...
you're the best!
KARAOKE NOW
Hooray!
groove
got the x-factor

Super Star Dad

You may not have a mega voice

Or wow us on guitar.

But, Dad, we are your biggest fans

And you're our Super Star!